Angel Finance

Portfolio Success and Startup Economics

Student Edition

Books by the Authors

Fundamentals of Angel Investing
A Guide to the Principles, Skills and Concepts Every Angel Investor Needs to Succeed

Angel Investing by the Numbers
Valuation, Capitalization, Portfolio Construction and Startup Economics

Leaders Wanted: Making Startup Deals Happen
Advanced Techniques in Deal Leadership and Due Diligence for Early Stage Investors

Guide, Advise and Inspire: How Startup Boards Drive Growth and Exits
An Overview of the Principles, Skills and Concepts Every Early Stage Company Board Member Needs to Succeed

Venture Capital: A Practical Guide
A Guide to Fund Formation and Management

Angel Investing Course Books by the Authors

Angel 101 and Angel 201
Introduction to Angel Investing

Due Diligence
Evaluating Investment Opportunities

Termsheets and Valuations
Negotiating Investments

Portfolio Success and Startup Economics
Angel Finance

Angel Finance

Portfolio Success and Startup Economics

Student Edition

Hambleton Lord

Christopher Mirabile

Seraf
Compass
Publications

www.seraf-investor.com

Copyright © 2018 by Seraf LLC

All rights reserved. No part of this publication may be reproduced, distributed, or transmitted in any form or by any means, including photocopying, recording, or other electronic or mechanical methods, without the prior written permission of the publisher, except in the case of brief quotations embodied in critical reviews and certain other noncommercial uses permitted by copyright law. For permission requests, contact the publisher, addressed "Attention: Permissions Coordinator," at the address below.

support@seraf-investor.com

www.seraf-investor.com

Cover Illustration Copyright: lublubachka / 123RF Stock Photo

Table of Contents

1. **Introduction - Angel Finance**   1

2. **Building Portfolio Success**   5
   - 2.1. Introduction   9
   - 2.2. Asset Allocation   11
   - 2.3. Investment Returns   17
   - 2.4. Portfolio Management   23
   - 2.5. Maximizing Your Returns   27
   - 2.6. Portfolio Success Resources   33

3. **Startup Economics: Capitalization and Exits**   39
   - 3.1. Introduction   43
   - 3.2. Financing Companies   45
   - 3.3. Capitalization Tables   49
   - 3.4. Types of Exits   57
   - 3.5. Timing and Planning Exits   63
   - 3.6. Alignment   69
   - 3.7. Startup Economics Resources   73

Appendix

I. Overview   79

II. Capitalization Tables with Waterfall Analysis   81

III. Sample IRS 83(b) Election Form   89

IV. Early Stage Investment Portfolio Modeling Tool   99

V. Exit Planning Guide   103

Introduction
Angel Finance

The sensational plays get the most attention. In the sport of Major League Baseball, the greatest hitters are those who get a hit just one out of every three times at bat and a home run 5 or 6 times out of 100 at bats. In the world of startup company investing, the best-known investors are those who invest in the tiny percentage of companies that make it big. Think Facebook, Google or Amazon. If you invest in one of those enormously successful companies you will find your name in the equivalent of the Baseball Hall of Fame… it's called the Forbes Midas List.

The most famous investors don't focus on their on-base percentage. In fact, their batting average might be quite low. They are so successful because they swing for the fences every time they get up to bat, and they are able to connect for the rare grand slam.

It is tempting to think that is the only way to succeed. And maybe if you are trying to build a reputation as the best home run hitter in baseball it is. But if you are trying to field a winning team over the course of a long season, it is not the only way, or even necessarily the best way.

The principles popularized by Michael Lewis' book MoneyBall outline a different and less dramatic way. An approach of chipping away at the problem, making every position and every at bat count for as much as it can. Efficiency and economy in playing style rather than flamboyance.

Angel Investing Approaches to Long Term Returns

So which is the right method for an angel looking for long term returns? Should a typical angel investor apply the "swing for the fences" approach to their personal investing? After all, if you make just one hugely successful investment in your portfolio, you will make up for dozens of failed investments. Sure, you can try that, particularly if you live in an ecosystem full of breakout consumer ideas, each with global potential.

But, the likelihood of investing in the biggest winners is quite low - too low to bank on. Further, some of the biggest winners come in the consumer space where there is a global market, but a lot of consumer fickleness. And some of the biggest winners are bolstered by access to tremendous depths of capital - VCs almost will them into market winners by brute force. Angels don't have the capital to do that, and when they rely on VCs to do it for them in later rounds, the dilution is often very detrimental to overall returns. When combined with the much longer time to "Unicorn" exit, it can combine to make for a anemic portfolio. Reliance on these kinds of deals has an element of risk it is almost impossible to be compensated for taking on.

Therefore, our personal strategy for angel investing isn't 100% focused on the hunt for the biggest winners. We are delighted when we find such investments, but we are realists and understand that, on a day-to-day, year-to-year basis, we need to take a different approach to building our angel investment portfolios. Our strategy is more akin to the MoneyBall "efficiency and economy" approach to investing. We don't try to wait for the perfect pitch and rely on grand slams, we try to accumulate lots of doubles, triples and the occasional home runs. If the bases happen to be loaded when we get one, great, but we don't bet the portfolio on it.

So how does this actually work in real life? We stay focused on investing in great teams, going after big markets with great new solutions to the customer's problem. But it goes beyond those basics. Even when you find a good opportunity, there are many mistakes you can make after your first check that will hurt, if not outright eliminate, your returns.

In these courses on Angel Finance, we will discuss what investors should know about the financial mechanics of angel investing. Just like the baseball team manager using a MoneyBall approach needs to really understand the statistics of the game, the successful investor employing our approach needs to understand the financial mechanics of investing.

What's in this Book?

There are two main sections in this book. The first section includes the slides for an in-depth, 2 hour class that we call "**Building Portfolio Success**". This class will introduce you to four key topics that all angel investors need to understand as they make investments and ultimately build a successful portfolio of early stage companies:
1. Asset Allocation: Portfolio Size, Risk and Diversification
2. Investment Returns: VC and Angel Returns, Capital Allocation Strategies
3. Portfolio Management: Portfolio Construction, Tracking and Exits
4. Maximizing Returns: Tax Issues and Board Compensation

The second section includes the slides for an in-depth, 2 hour class that we call "**Startup Economics: Capitalization and Exits**". In this course, we dig deep into helping you understand how early stage companies are financed from inception to successful exit. The course will provide detailed material in five main areas:
1. Financing Companies: Key Milestones, Long Term Financing Plans
2. Capitalization Tables
3. Types of Exits
4. Timing and Planning Exits
5. Alignment: Keeping Investors and Management Aligned

In addition to these two slide decks, we include an appendix with tools and guides that help investors improve their returns. In the appendix you will find:
1. Capitalization Tables with Waterfall Analysis
2. Early Stage Investment Portfolio Modeling Tool
3. Exit Planning Guide
4. Sample IRS 83(b) Election Form

By mastering the materials in this book, you should be confident that you can understand the financial economics of a successful startup and ways in which to construct a profitable early stage company portfolio.

ANGEL FINANCE

Building Portfolio Success

Angel Capital Association
World's Largest Association of Active Accredited Investors

ABOUT US

Vision

ACA is recognized as the trusted authority in angel investing.

- 13,000+ Investors
- 250+ Organizations
- Every US State and 5 Canadian Provinces
- Individual Angels, Angel Groups, Accredited Platforms, Family Offices

---

1 EVENTS
Host many international, national and regional events a year

2 EDUCATION
Provide gold standard education for angels

3 PUBLIC POLICY
Leading voice for angels on public policy lobbying in Washington, DC

4 DATA & RESEARCH
Central resource for angel investing data and research

Our Mission

Fuel the success of the accredited investor community through advocacy, education and connection building.

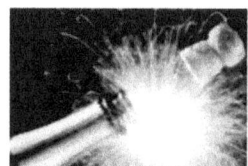

Welcome Message

Seraf's Philosophy

We believe investors in early stage companies should have access to best practices and professional tools to support the entrepreneurial community worldwide and achieve superior outcomes.

Insights and education, combined with powerful portfolio management tools allow investors to understand their investing better, learn faster and make necessary adjustments to select the highest quality opportunities and drive superior returns.

About the Authors

Ham is Co-Founder of Seraf and the Chairman of Launchpad Venture Group, a Boston-based angel group. Through his involvement with Launchpad, Ham has built a personal portfolio of 50+ early stage investments. In addition, he is a board member or board observer with 5 early stage companies.

Christopher is Chair Emeritus of the Angel Capital Association and Managing Director of Launchpad Venture Group. He helps manage Launchpad's portfolio of 70+ companies, he has personally invested in over 65 start-up companies, and is a limited partner in four specialized angel funds. Christopher is a board member, advisor and mentor to numerous start-ups, and a frequent panelist and speaker on entrepreneurship and angel-related topics.

Seraf Co-Founders
Ham Lord & Christopher Mirabile

Presentation Overview

1 INTRODUCTION
Financial Mechanics of Angel Investing

2 ASSET ALLOCATION
Portfolio Size, Risk & Diversification

3 INVESTMENT RETURNS
VC & Angel Returns, Capital Allocation Strategies

4 PORTFOLIO MANAGEMENT
Portfolio Construction, Tracking & Exits

5 MAXIMIZING YOUR RETURNS
Taxes Issues, Board Compensation

6 APPENDIX
Tools and Forms

Building a Successful Angel Portfolio

In the world of venture capital, the best-known VCs invest in the big winners (e.g. Amazon, Google, etc.)

VCs focus on high-growth, huge-market companies with a chance at $1B+ exits

Is "swinging for the fences" the best approach for angel investors?

Or, are there other approaches that angels can apply which result in top tier financial returns?

Moneyball and Sabermetrics teach us that base hits can be as important as home runs.

The Financial Mechanics of Angel Investing

In this course, we will look to answer the following key questions:

- How do you construct a portfolio to improve the likelihood of successful returns and minimize capital risk?
- What are some financial paths companies take that lead to a successful exit for angel investors?
- What does the financial return look like in a top tier angel portfolio?
- What can angels do to minimize taxes and improve their financial outcome?

If you don't know where you are going, you probably won't get there.

ANGEL FINANCE
Asset Allocation

How Much Should I Invest?

Consider angel investing as part of your overall **asset allocation strategy**

- Public Company Stock, Real Estate, Collectables, Commodities
- Hedge Funds, Private Equity, Venture Capital

Illiquid private company investments (e.g. Angel Investments, VC) should represent a **minority percent** of your asset allocation

For the majority of angel investors, a 5% to 10% allocation to angel investments is sufficient and prudent

Don't put more into angel investing than you can afford to lose.

How Many Investments Should I Make?

Diversification is a core feature of almost all successful angel portfolios
- You need to make a minimum of 10 investments
- But, diversification begins, not ends, at 10 companies - 20+ investments will greatly increase your likelihood of a positive overall return

One 10X return will pay for 9 mistakes.

Are There Other Diversification Factors?

Consider building a portfolio with companies that are in different:

- Industries or sectors
- Stages of development
- Types of entrepreneurs
- Types of key risks

Invest in a few companies which allow you to be involved and leverage your expertise, and invest in some where you can afford to be more passive.

Macro-economic cycles vary, as do industry cycles - a large and diverse portfolio will insulate you from business cycle swings.

How Do I Pace My Angel Investing?

Here is what it takes to build a portfolio of 10 to 20 companies:

- 3 to 5 new investments per year for initial 4 years
- Follow-on investments equalling $1 for every $1 invested in each company
- With $10K checks, you will invest between $30K and $100K per year
- Total amount invested will range between $200K and $400K

To the brand new angel looking to put $75K into their first deal, I say "how about $10K into seven deals? You'll thank me someday..."

How Do I Evaluate Risk vs. Return?

In every asset class, you are looking to understand overall risk vs. return

Can you recognize opportunities with the potential to deliver excess returns for the risks presented?

Experienced angel investors tend to prefer **execution** type risks rather than **technical or science** risks

Will you be a low conviction angel with a "Spray and Pray" approach, or a high conviction angel with a more concentrated portfolio?

What's an Appropriate Return Given the Risks?

Angel investments are zero liquidity, long term, high risk investments

Therefore, returns should be higher than liquid investments like public stocks

So, what should the return premium over public company stocks be?
- 5%, 10%, more?

To understand likely returns, you need to analyze the capital structure, future capital requirements, and the exit potential for the company.

What Types of Rounds Can I Invest In?

Growth consumes cash; companies tend to raise more than once
- Seed rounds are the earliest independent money
- Mainstream angel rounds are typically $250K-$2.5M
- Later rounds may be Angel, VC or both

If things are going well, later rounds are merely arithmetically dilutive; if things are going poorly, they are economically AND arithmetically dilutive.

Should I Invest in an Early Seed Round?

Early seed rounds are hard to price and typically overvalue the company

- Risk/Reward ratio is often *better* in the *later* rounds
- But, by making an initial investment, you gain the option to invest in future rounds

The price of admission in the hottest deals is often the small check you wrote in the early seed round.

What is a Follow-on Round?

Most startups have a continuous need for funds to help grow the business

- "Follow-on" financings typically occur 9 to 15 months after prior round
- Investors can choose whether to participate or not in the new round

Investing early in a company's history gives you a front row seat to observe how the company progresses and how the team grows.

What Factors Affect Follow-on Investments?

With your first investment, you are buying an informational advantage

- As winners become apparent, make **offensive** investments to maintain your ownership
- For companies that struggle, make small **defensive** investments to protect your ownership

Over time, a successful portfolio allocation strategy will end up with more capital invested in the winners than in the losers!

ANGEL FINANCE
Investment Returns

Perspective on Venture Capital Returns

Venture Capital returns are closely monitored and reported upon by firms such as Cambridge Associates and Thomson Reuters

- Recent reports indicates top quartile funds delivered an annual return between 15% and 27% (approx $3 returned for every $1 invested)
- Bottom quartile funds had returns in the low single digit percentages

Top performing institutional venture funds consistently outperform the S&P 500. Unfortunately, the majority of venture funds aren't top performers.

Angel Investing Returns

Angel Investing returns are more challenging to track

There have been multiple research efforts based on limited data

- Largest and most formal report (2007) by Wiltbank and Boeker using 3,097 investments from 538 angels... Shows a 27% annual rate of return

More research and data is needed to better understand angel returns. The ACA Data Analytics Project is focused on this research.

How to Improve Angel Investing Returns

Wiltbank / Boeker study indicates that angel returns are better when angels:

- Put in 20-40 hours of diligence
- Had expertise or access to expertise
- Interacted with portfolio companies with coaching, connections, etc.

A risky, illiquid and labor-intensive asset class had better offer superior returns!

Distribution of Company Exits - Multiples

Right-Skewed Distribution of US Venture Returns

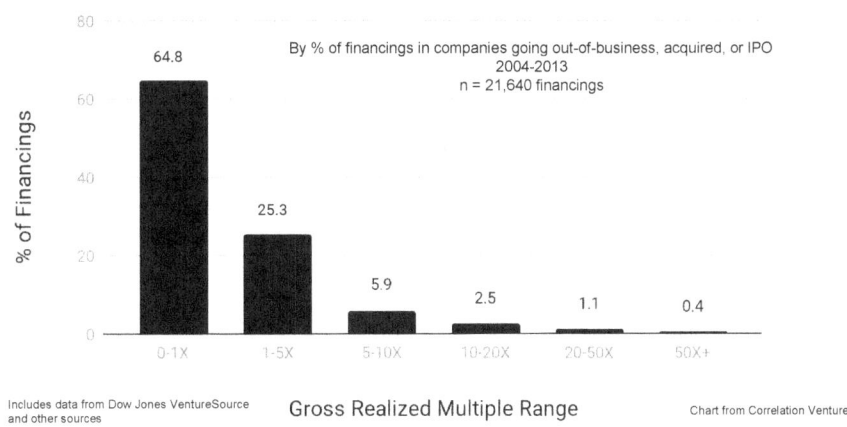

By % of financings in companies going out-of-business, acquired, or IPO
2004-2013
n = 21,640 financings

Includes data from Dow Jones VentureSource and other sources. Chart from Correlation Ventures.

Less than 1 out of 20 venture-backed companies turns into a home run.

Distribution of Company Exits - Dollars

2016 Global Tech Exits

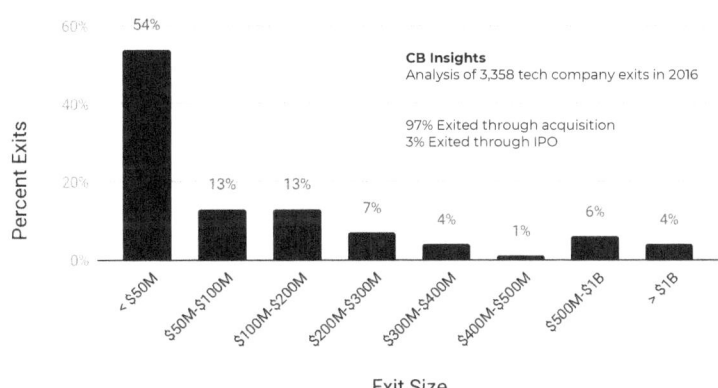

CB Insights
Analysis of 3,358 tech company exits in 2016

97% Exited through acquisition
3% Exited through IPO

These exits only include VC exits. There are many more exits of angel backed companies in the sub $50M range.

Are VCs Interested in $50M Exits?

The short answer to the question is "No"

The long answer to the question involves a bit of math…

- A Top Quartile $100M Venture Fund should return $250M+
- Using standard assumptions on a venture fund capital allocation, successful companies in the fund must exit at greater than $200M

If a VC can only model a $50M exit as a best case scenario for a company, they are looking at a $10M return to the fund

It's hard for a VC to justify the time and effort of putting such a small investment into their fund.

What is a VC's Capital Allocation Strategy?

Primary Goal: return at least 2.5-3X the total capital invested in their fund

How can they achieve this goal?

- Look for 5X to 10X+ multiples on invested capital
- Only invest in companies with exit potential greater than $200M
- Reserve capital for top performers in their portfolios
- Protect downside with liquidation preferences and dividends

A well managed venture fund focuses on companies with the greatest potential exit and understands how to allocate capital to increase overall fund returns.

Angels: A Different Approach to Capitalization

Angels do well when investing in smaller ($20M - $50M) opportunities, if the company:

- Is properly capitalized (raises $1M - $3M of equity capital)
- Is able to execute to plan and avoid expensive pivots
- Hits key metrics that create real value interesting to buyers
- Has multiple exit opportunities (strategic and financial buyers)

You can make money in any kind of exit, provided the companies capitalization is appropriate for the exit.

What Can Angels Do to Minimize Capital Risk?

Invest in capital efficient companies - they are a great fit for angels

Make sure you reserve sufficient funds for follow-on rounds in more capital intensive companies

Work with founders and board to assure alignment on long-term capital plan

Help founders select co-investors with similar capital strategies

VCs have depth of capital that must be put to work; angels don't. Angels thrive where VCs can't, in more capital efficient companies headed for mainstream exits.

ANGEL FINANCE
Portfolio Management

Building a Successful Angel Portfolio

If you build a portfolio of 10+ companies, what can you expect?

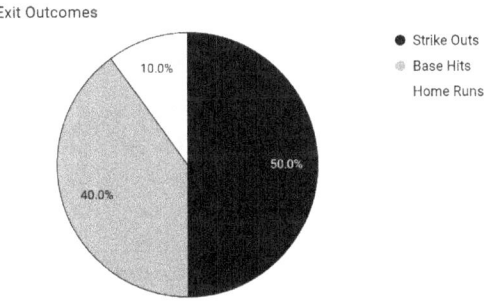

If you don't perform due diligence and add human capital to support your investments, you limit your chance of achieving these results.

How Do You Get a 3X Return on Your Capital?

There are **many paths** to a 3X return

Here's one example where we invest the same amount ($1) in each of 10 companies:

- 5 companies fail and return $1 in total
- 3 companies are small exits and return $9 (~$3 from each)
- 1 company is a medium exit and returns $5
- 1 company is a home run and returns $15

If you add up the returns, it equals $30 for your $10 of invested capital

Without one 10X+ home run in your portfolio, it's extremely difficult to achieve a 3X return.

Pathways to a Successful Angel Exit

Successful exits for private companies come in many different flavors

- **Early Exit**: Most likely a 2x-4x return
- **Dividend or Royalty**: Good way to get your invested capital back and continue to hold stock for a future payout
- **Share Buy-Out**: Large VCs are willing to purchase stock from existing shareholders to increase their ownership
- **Large Acquisition**: Type of exit where angels make most of their returns
- **IPO**: A rare event you will brag about forever!

No matter which path the company heads down, it can't be left to random chance. Building a solid exit strategy takes planning.

How Long Will It Take Before an Exit?

From the time you invest in a seed round till the company has an exit can vary quite a bit:

- **Early Exit**: Typically happens within 1 to 3 years
- **Dividend or Royalty**: Company needs to be generating profits - usually takes 4+ years
- **Share Buy-Out**: Company needs to grow rapidly in huge market - as early as 2 to 4 years
- **Large Acquisition**: Building a big business takes time - at least 7 years
- **IPO**: Recent history tells us this will take 10+ years

With exits, if you let perfect be the enemy of good, you may be in for a long wait...

Should I Manage My Angel Investments?

Yes. Serious angels need to do something to get an overview of their portfolio and separate the forest from the trees. A good portfolio management solution will allow you to easily:

- **Record**: Keep transaction records
- **Analyze**: Automatically calculate returns metrics
- **Track**: Review quarterly reports from companies
- **Monitor**: Track key dates and actions (e.g. warrant expirations)
- **Optimize**: Maximize tax efficiency to improve portfolio returns
- **Share**: Have the ability to share your records with advisors / family

Investors use sophisticated solutions from Fidelity/Schwab/etc. to manage public investments. Shouldn't they use tools to manage their private investments, too?

ANGEL FINANCE
Maximizing Your Returns

What US Tax Rules Apply to Angel Investing?

The key tax rules that offer significant benefits to US-based angels include:

Wins: IRS Sections 1202 & 1045 provide benefits when you have capital gains

Losses: IRS Section 1244 provides benefits when you have capital losses

Your Companies: Huge R&D Tax credits available even to unprofitable companies - can be applied to payroll taxes

IRS tax rules are subject to change. Make sure you have an accountant familiar with tax rules for investments in Qualified Small Business Stock (QSBS).

IRS Section 1202

Section 1202 allows for the exclusion of capital gains on stock

- You can exclude up to the greater of $10M or 10 times your investment
- You must hold the stock for at least 5 years

- Stock acquired between 8/10/93 and 2/17/09:   50% Exclusion
- Stock acquired between 2/18/09 and 9/27/10:   75% Exclusion
- Stock acquired after 9/28/10:   100% Exclusion

Angels should make a 1202 & 1244 review a fixed part of every years tax checklist

IRS Section 1045

Section 1045 allows you to avoid paying capital gains if:

- You put all of your gains into a new QSBS investment
- You make the new investment within 60 days of the sale

The holding period of the new investment includes the holding period of the stock you just sold (helps with 1202)

Be careful… don't let the tax tail wag the investment dog by jumping into an impulsive investment!

IRS Section 1244

This provision in the tax code comes into play on capital losses

In most situations, you will write off capital losses vs. your capital gains

However, Section 1244 allows you to write off losses vs. the higher earned income tax rate if you are part of the first $1M invested in a QSBS company

Make sure you record whether you are part of the initial $1M invested in a company at time of investment. It can be very difficult to document this after a company goes out of business.

Additional Returns from Board Service?

Unlike VCs, Angels who take board seats typically receive some form of compensation due to the following reasons:

- Representing and working on behalf of many individual investors
- Volunteering time and not being paid a fund management fee or carry
- Angels are typically relatively small shareholders, so board compensation can make a real economic difference

Angels are helping the company with skills, connections and expertise at a very early stage when help from a board is sorely needed.

How Are Angel Directors Compensated?

Almost always in the form of equity rather than cash

Initial grant is an amount between 0.25% and 1% of company's total shares

Typically paid as follows:

- Stock Options or Restricted Stock
- Initial grant at the time of joining the board
- Supplementary grants given in future years

An equity grant can be a big multiplier on your investment return - doubling or tripling your cash-on-cash return in a good outcome.

Forms of Payment for Director Compensation

Stock Options: You don't own the stock till it vests and you exercise the options

Restricted Stock: The stock is granted up front, but subject to restrictions which fall away over time

Options have ownership rights which vest over time, and restricted shares have ownership restrictions which lapse over time.

Tax Planning For Restricted Stock

Key difference between stock options and restricted stock is potential tax efficiency

Restricted stock tax benefits are due to IRS Section 83(b) election option

- Grantee declares income from restricted stock on date of grant
- Due to relatively low fair market value of restricted common stock in an early stage company, the income tax payment will be small
- And, the clock starts on capital gains treatment of any future profit, including IRS Section 1202 tax benefits

Make sure you ask the company CEO for restricted stock and do the 83b election. If the company has a successful exit, you will save a lot of money on your taxes.

Tax Planning For Stock Options

Options received by non-management board directors are non-qualified

To take advantage of capital gains treatment, you must:

- Wait for the stock to vest
- Pay the exercise price on vested stock
- Pay tax on the income that is imputed from the difference between the exercise price and the fair market value of the shares
- Start the holding period for capital gains treatment

Plan ahead to avoid exercising all of your options at the time of company exit. You don't want to pay the ordinary income tax rate on the whole transaction.

ANGEL FINANCE
Appendix

Resources - Modeling Tool for Early Stage Investment Portfolios

A successful early stage investment portfolio has a mix of strikeouts, base hits and home runs. So how is it possible for an early stage investor to build a successful portfolio compiled from companies that produce such widely different financial returns? To answer that question, we pulled together a simple modeling tool that helps you visualize how the probable returns play out and interact to produce an overall portfolio return.

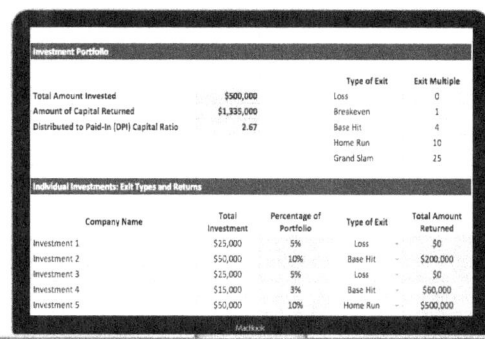

Download
Modeling Tool
bit.ly/Seraf_Portfolio_Modeling_Tool

Resources - IRS 83(b) Election Form

Filing an 83(b) Election is not that complicated, but it does require a fair number of steps and it must be done in a very timely fashion. The first thing to be aware of is you must file your 83(b) Election within 30 days of receiving the grant. That's not much time to get your paperwork filed, but those are the rules!

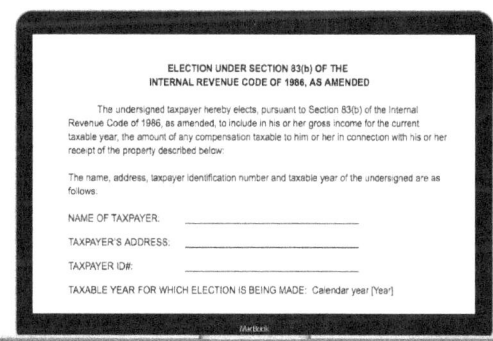

Download
IRS 83(b) Election Form
bit.ly/IRSsection83bElectionForm

The Seraf Compass

Continue Your Angel Education and Improve Your Investing Skills

The Seraf Compass guides early stage investors in making better investing decisions, minimizing risk and improving returns

Angel Finance Articles

bit.ly/AngelInvestingByTheNumbers

Angel Finance eBook

bit.ly/ByTheNumbersEbook

Angel Finance Hardcopy Book

bit.ly/HardCopyBooks

Angel Finance Tools

bit.ly/SerafToolbox

The Seraf Compass

From Investment to Exit: Insights, news, thought leadership and in-depth resources for early stage investors

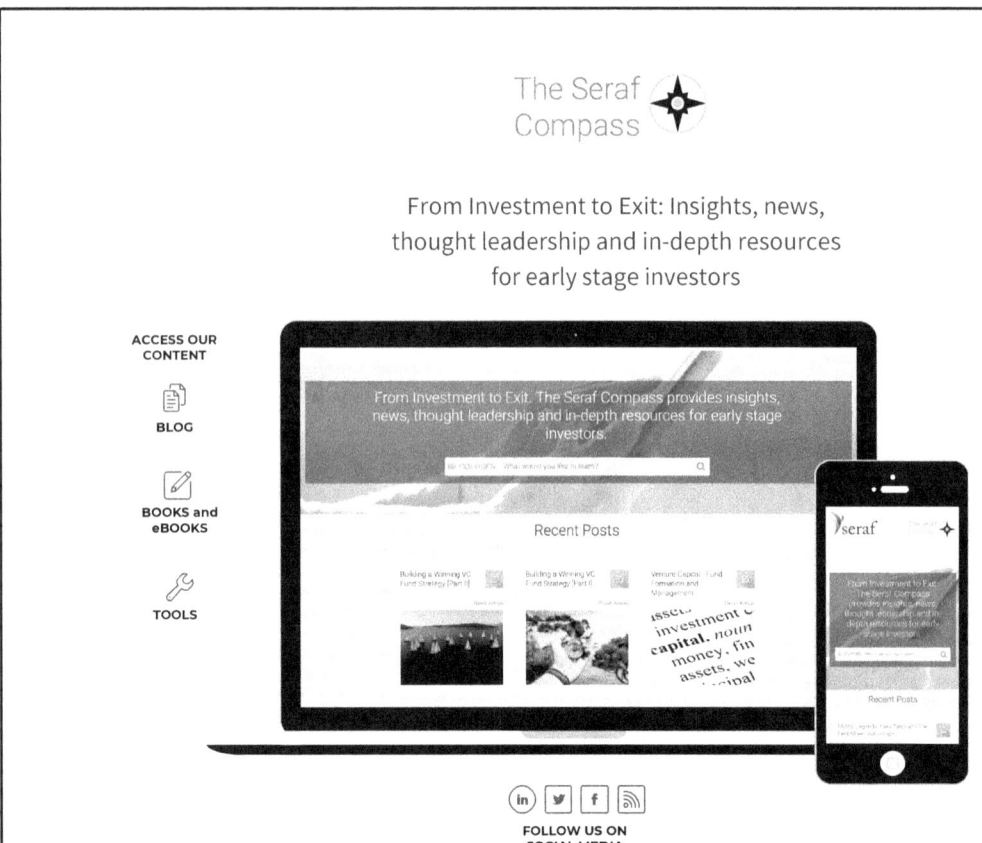

ACCESS OUR CONTENT
- BLOG
- BOOKS and eBOOKS
- TOOLS

FOLLOW US ON SOCIAL MEDIA

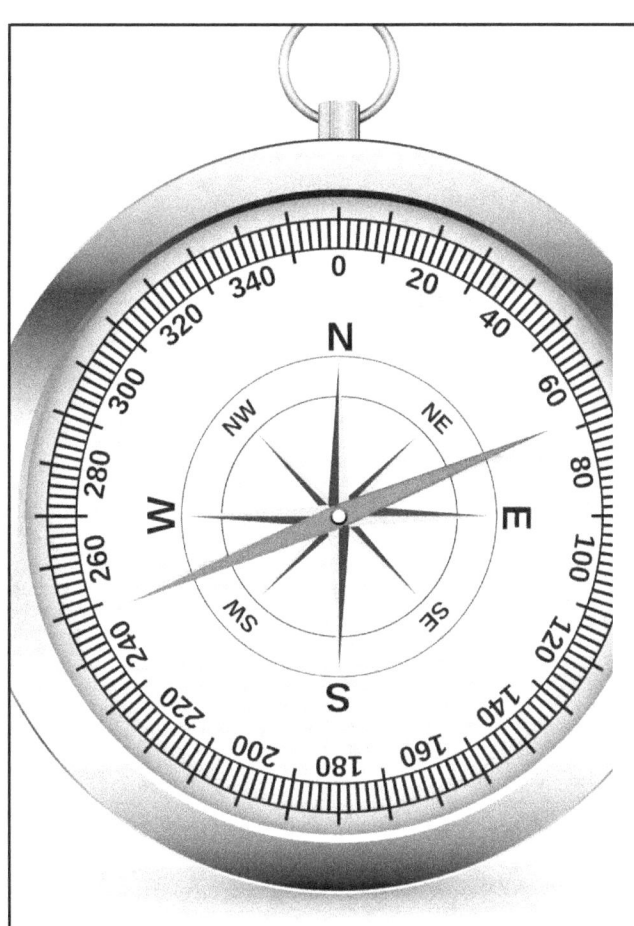

Books from Seraf

Fundamentals of Angel Investing
A Guide to the Principles, Skills and Concepts Every Angel Investor Needs to Succeed

Angel Investing by the Numbers
Valuation, Capitalization, Portfolio Construction and Startup Economics

Leaders Wanted: Making Startup Deals Happen
Advanced Techniques in Deal Leadership and Due Diligence for Early Stage Investors

Guide, Advise and Inspire: How Startup Boards Drive Growth and Exits
An Overview of the Principles, Skills and Concepts Every Early Stage Company Board Member Needs to Succeed

Venture Capital: A Practical Guide
A Guide to Fund Formation and Management

PORTFOLIO MANAGEMENT FOR EARLY STAGE INVESTORS

All Your Info. One Place. Smart Investing.

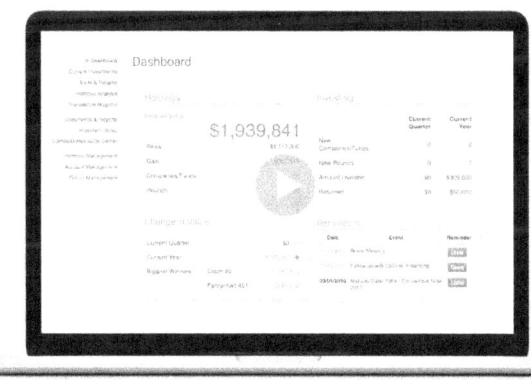

WHAT MAKES SERAF DIFFERENT

Easy Workflow
Seraf guides you through a few easy steps to get your portfolio up and running quickly. Get an overview, develop insights and generate reports in no time.

Deep Experience
Designed by active, early stage investors with over 25 years experience in fund creation and management, the Seraf team understands the complexities of today's early stage investment landscape.

Uniquely Focused Solution
Developed specifically to meet the needs of early stage investors, Seraf provides the tools YOU need to manage your portfolio efficiently.

AUTHORS

Hambleton Lord

Christopher Mirabile

CONTACT US

www.seraf-investor.com

www.angelcapitalassociation.org

ANGEL FINANCE

Startup Economics: Capitalization and Exits

Angel Capital Association
World's Largest Association of Active Accredited Investors

ABOUT US

Vision

ACA is recognized as the trusted authority in angel investing.

- 13,000+ Investors
- 250+ Organizations
- Every US State and 5 Canadian Provinces
- Individual Angels, Angel Groups, Accredited Platforms, Family Offices

★ Full Members
★ Provisional Members
★ Affiliates
★ Accredited Platform

---

1 EVENTS
Host many international, national and regional events a year

2 EDUCATION
Provide gold standard education for angels

3 PUBLIC POLICY
Leading voice for angels on public policy lobbying in Washington, DC

4 DATA & RESEARCH
Central resource for angel investing data and research

Our Mission

Fuel the success of the accredited investor community through advocacy, education and connection building.

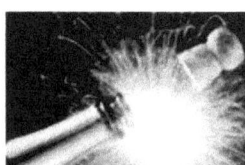

The American Angel

Welcome Message

Seraf's Philosophy

We believe investors in early stage companies should have access to best practices and professional tools to support the entrepreneurial community worldwide and achieve superior outcomes.

Insights and education, combined with powerful portfolio management tools allow investors to understand their investing better, learn faster and make necessary adjustments to select the highest quality opportunities and drive superior returns.

About the Authors

Ham is Co-Founder of Seraf and the Chairman of Launchpad Venture Group, a Boston-based angel group. Through his involvement with Launchpad, Ham has built a personal portfolio of 50+ early stage investments. In addition, he is a board member or board observer with 5 early stage companies.

Christopher is Chair Emeritus of the Angel Capital Association and Managing Director of Launchpad Venture Group. He helps manage Launchpad's portfolio of 70+ companies, he has personally invested in over 65 start-up companies, and is a limited partner in four specialized angel funds. Christopher is a board member, advisor and mentor to numerous start-ups, and a frequent panelist and speaker on entrepreneurship and angel-related topics.

 Seraf Co-Founders
Ham Lord & Christopher Mirabile

Presentation Overview

1 INTRODUCTION
Financial pathways to startup success

2 FINANCING COMPANIES
Key milestones, long term financing plans

3 CAPITALIZATION TABLES
Who owns what

4 TYPES OF EXITS
The Good, the Bad and the Ugly

5 TIMING & PLANNING EXITS
Finding the right buyer

6 ALIGNMENT
Keeping investors and management aligned

7 APPENDIX
Guides and tools

Financial Pathways to Startup Success

Successfully investing in startups takes planning and forethought

Planning involves analysis of long term capital pathways and how they relate to exit outcomes

This requires an understanding of financing stacks, capitalization tables, exit types and exit planning

Angels can make money in any exit, provided the capitalization plan is appropriate for the exit.

The Financial Mechanics of a Startup

In this course, we will look to answer the following key questions:

- How do you align company milestones with a long term financing plan?
- How do you read and understand a Capitalization Table?
- What financial paths lead to successful exits for angel investors?
- How do you plan for an acquisition and what does the timing look like?
- How do you keep management and investors in alignment?

ANGEL FINANCE
Financing Companies

Key Milestones in Startup Financing

Investor Type	Financing	Company Stage, Milestones Achieved
Founders, Grants, Incubators, Friends & Family	Pre-Seed ($100-$250K)	1 or 2 Passionate Founders, Product Prototype
Angels, Micro VCs	Seed ($250K-$2.5M)	Small team, early customer interest, promising market opportunity
Early Stage VCs, Corporate VCs	Series A & B ($2M-$10M)	Established product/market fit, management team filling out, rapid growth (75%+ annually)
Late Stage VCs, Institutional Investors	Series C, etc. ($10M+)	Growing rapidly in huge market, expanding in new geographies, introducing new products
Public Markets	IPO ($100M+)	Seasoned management team, proven path to profitability and long term future growth

Startups have to walk before they run. Each new layer added to the capital stack changes assumptions and expectations.

How Big Should a Round Be?

First and foremost, understand what milestones can be achieved with the capital raised

Second, understand the significance of those milestones

- Will they increase the value of the company and your investment?
- Will new investors be interested in continuing to finance the company towards a successful exit?

Raise any money increases your post money valuation. Raise enough to be able to grow into that valuation or you are headed down a dead end.

What Is a Long Term Financing Plan?

Aligning total capital raised with market opportunity is critical:

- Very few companies have the potential for a $1B+ exit
- 80%+ of successful VC-backed exits are less than $200M
- The average (and majority of) M&A transactions are below $50M

Understanding the potential size of the exit for a successful startup is critical in building a long term financing plan that works out well for the entrepreneur and the investors.

Changing the Long Term Financing Plan

What factors affect the decision to move from a lightly financed company (e.g. < $5M) to a heavily financed company (e.g. > $10M)?

- **Team**: Does the CEO have a team that can execute on a much bigger scale?
- **Market Size**: Has the company found new, big opportunities?
- **Competition**: Can the company protect its advantages from aggressive competitors?

With big rounds, it is a be careful what you wish for situation: its the "3 Ps." "Potential" goes way up, but so does "period" and exit "probability" goes down.

Dangers of Undercapitalization

Being lightly financed isn't easy:

- **Sales**: A small team is challenged closing a large pipeline of business
- **Engineering**: Early product feature lead starts to diminish to better funded competitors
- **Marketing**: Maintaining market awareness is a long term battle that only increases as companies go after mainstream customers

Customer revenue is the cheapest financing; if a company is scrappy, ruthlessly efficient, and patient, it can deliver a big win with a small exit.

What are Showstopper Financing Issues?

Markets that are too small to model a 10X return for your investment

Capital-intensive businesses that require a $200M+ exit for a 10X return... here are the questions you need answers to:

- Who are the buyers and will they pay a price > $200M?
- What are the characteristics of recent exits in this market?
- Can this CEO deliver?

Outside capital is like a loan the acquirer is expected to pay back. If you cannot point to the likely acquirer, then don't expect to be paid back.

Dating Game for Early Stage Capital

Different types of investors have different:

- Motivations, Needs, Concerns
- Roles & Value-add
- Stages, Milestones and Round Sizes
- Risk/Return expectations

Understanding how different investors work, and finding right investors for company stage and trajectory is key to keeping everyone happy and everything moving smoothly

An investment relationship is like a marriage - check long term compatibility before committing.

ANGEL FINANCE
Capitalization Tables

What is a Capitalization Table?

Comprehensive document that includes a record for all stakeholders

Tracks both equity ownership and outstanding debt

- Common and preferred stock
- Stock options and warrants
- Convertible debt

The cap table is one of the most critical documents maintained by a company. It's vital for angels to understand it.

An Example Capitalization Table

Name	Common Stock	Stock Options	Series A Preferred	Total Shares	Percent Out-standing	Percent Fully Diluted
Founder One	1,500,000		250,000	1,750,000	47.0%	43.7%
Founder Two	1,100,000			1,100,000	29.6%	27.5%
Employee One		80,000		80,000	2.2%	2.0%
Employee Two		40,000		40,000	1.1%	1.0%
Investor One			500,000	500,000	13.4%	12.5%
Investor Two			250,000	250,000	6.7%	6.3%
Remaining Option Pool		280,000		280,000		7.0%
Total	2,600,000	400,000	1,000,000	4,000,000	100%	100%
Percent Ownership	65%	10%	25%	100%		

Key Cap Table Terms - Valuations

Pre-Money Valuation - Valuation placed on company prior to an investment made in company

Post-Money Valuation - Effective valuation of company after an investment is made in company

Price per Share - Calculation based on taking post-money valuation and dividing it by the number of fully diluted shares

Post-money = Pre-Money + Money Raised
Price per Share = Post-Money/Total Shares
Percent Owned = Money Raised/Post-Money

Key Cap Table Terms - Security Types

Common Stock - Most basic form of equity ownership in a company is called common stock

Preferred Stock - A class or series of stock with special rights and privileges. Preferred stock is paid before common (but after debt) during a sale

Convertible Preferred Stock - Preferred stock which has option to either accept repayment preference OR convert to common stock (and be paid at the same time and rate as common) under a specified set of circumstances

Key Cap Table Terms - Security Types

Non-participating Preferred - Preferred stock which has the right to be paid a multiple of original purchase price **OR** convert to common stock and "participate" in distribution to common

Participating Preferred - Preferred stock which has right to be paid original price (or more) **AND THEN** convert to common stock and "participate" in distribution to common as if it had simply converted in the first place

Key Cap Table Terms - Security Types

Stock Options - Contractual right to purchase specified number of shares for a specified price at a specified future date or dates

Warrants - Nearly the same as options, but unlike options, warrants are typically one-offs and not issued under the terms of the stock option plan

Restricted Stock - Restricted stock has ownership restrictions which lapse over time. They are similar to stock options but have tax efficiency features

Key Cap Table Terms - Share Counts

Authorized Shares - Number of shares duly authorized by company's board for present or future issuance

Outstanding Shares - Total number of shares issued -- only includes options and warrants that have been exercised

Fully Diluted Shares - Includes all granted options, restricted stock, warrants and often remainder of the option pool

How Does a Cap Table Change Over Time?

As company routinely adds employees, directors and advisors, it will:

- Establish an option pool or increase size of current pool
- Option pool should represent 5% to 25% of fully diluted shares
- Grant options and restricted stock from the option pool

Total shares outstanding is never static - options and restricted stock are constantly granted, vested, exercised. If precision is required, get an uptodate cap table.

How Does a Cap Table Change Over Time?

As company raises both equity and debt, it will:

- Sell new shares or derivatives of an existing security (e.g. common shares or options, warrants or restricted common)
- Sell new shares of a new security (e.g. preferred shares)
- Issue convertible debt
- Issue warrants as part of either a debt or equity round

Debt that doesn't convert to equity is not an official part of the equity capitalization, but it should be tracked in the Cap Table to understand how payments will be made to shareholders upon sale of the company.

Do Convertible Notes Affect the Cap Table?

Convertible notes are a type of debt that is meant to be paid back via conversion into shares of the company

Terms of conversion to shares can be complicated, so make sure you know how much convertible debt is outstanding and what terms apply to it.

In almost all liquidation situations, debt holders are paid first before proceeds are paid to equity holders.

Effect of Liquidation Preference on Cap Table

Right to be paid "in preference to" (i.e. before) all other junior classes of stock

Can specify your preference as 1X your money, or a higher number such as 1.5X or 2X

Multiple liquidation preferences (i.e. higher than 1X) can mean death for early investors. You might think you want them on your $1M round until someone comes along wanting them on their $10M round.

Effect of Anti-Dilution Provision on Cap Table

Automatic retroactive adjustment of stock purchase price if there is a future down round

Typically effectuated by issuing additional stock to original buyers

Alternative approaches to calculating how much remedy to apply:
- Broad-based weighted average
- Narrow-based weighted average
- Full-ratchet

Anti-dilution protection is cold comfort: if you need it things are probably not going well for the company, plus the founder economics may be destroyed.

Effect of Dividend on Cap Table

Dividends may specify they are paid in preference to common

Can be authorized but not paid except in certain trigger conditions

May specify a set rate; May or may not be cumulative

A dividend accumulating in the background can make an enormous difference in the ultimate returns of different classes of stock.

What is a Waterfall Analysis?

Technical term used to describe process of calculating exact amounts each equity and debt holder will be paid upon company exit

- A series of sequential calculations
- Factors in various deal terms for all types of equity and debt

Last money in is usually first money out, so you have to run the waterfall to figure out how much will be left for early rounds and common.

ANGEL FINANCE
Types of Exits

Type of Exits

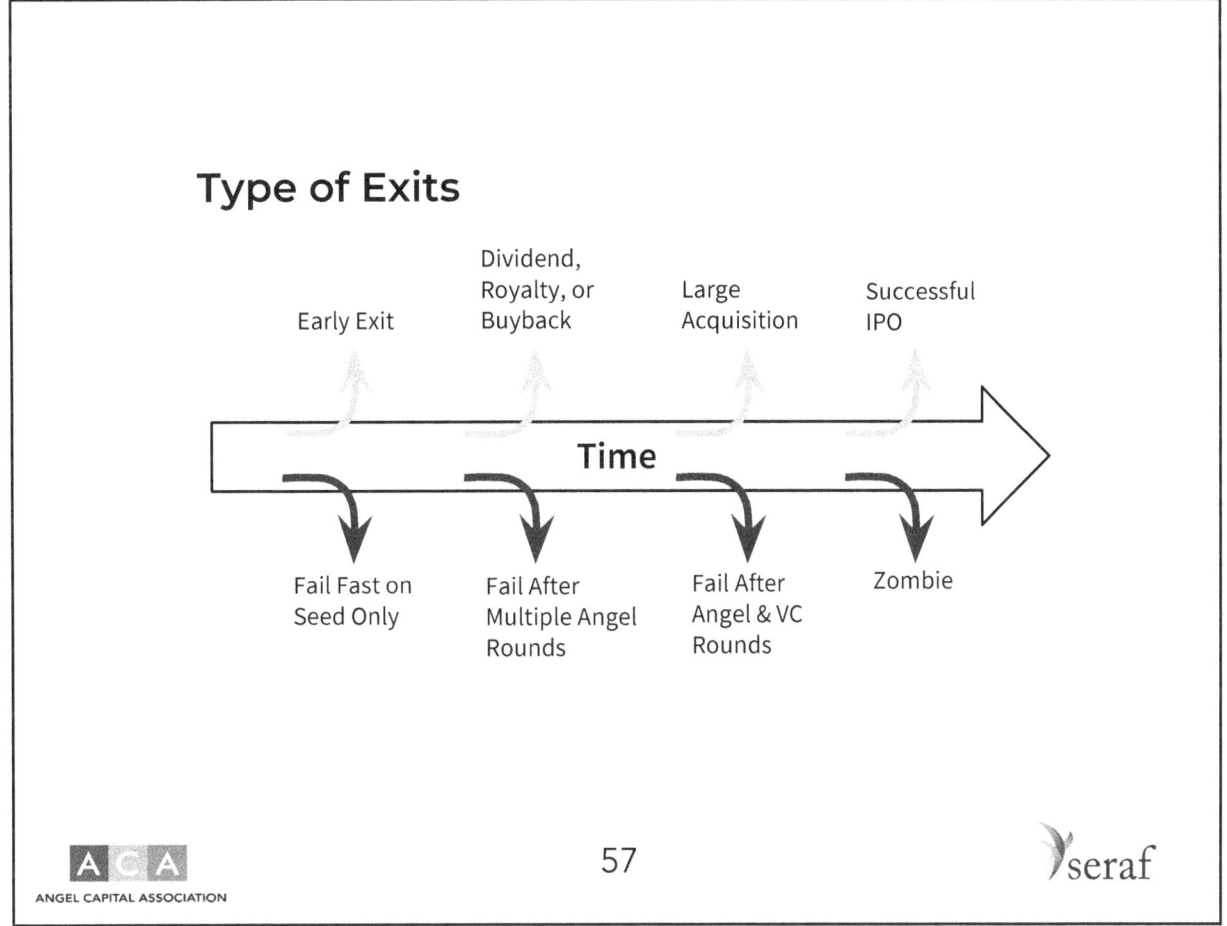

Fail Fast on Seed Only

Usually characterized as an interesting idea that didn't pan out

Company raised small amount of capital, but:

- Product didn't work as expected, or
- Customers weren't that interested in buying, or
- Team didn't work well together

Remember: the only thing worse than a mistake, is an expensive mistake.

Fail After Multiple Angel Rounds

Most common scenario for failed angel deals

- Company makes some early progress, but needs more capital
- One bridge round turns into two or three additional rounds
- Company continues to underachieve on business plan
- Investor fatigue sets in and company can't raise new financing
- The result is a fire sale of company's remaining assets

This scenario highlights the human tendency to not want to admit you were wrong until absolutely forced to.

Fail After Angel and VC Rounds

Some of the most promising startups end up in this bucket

- You invest in seed round and company gets early traction
- VCs take interest and company raises Series A at good valuation
- Initial success doesn't pan out, growth stalls and company pivots
- New financing is needed resulting in heavy dilution to investors
- Company is sold at a modest price, returning little if any capital to early investors

This is the kind of investment where having a careful follow-on decision making process can help your "average $ into winners" exceed your "average $ into losers."

Zombies

Most (if not all) experienced angels have at least one of these investments

- Business grows slowly but surely, revenues climb into low millions
- Company can stay in business - it is at or near cash flow breakeven
- But, it's too slow growing for VCs and too small for acquirers
- Founders aren't motivated to sell - they have a lifestyle company

If you are an investor in a company that fits this description, get together with other investors and work with the CEO to come up with an exit plan.

Early Exits

Positive early exits happen when a company's new product:

- Complements a fast growing acquirer's product line
- Has potential to damage acquirer's market position
- Fills new emerging gap in acquirer's product line
- Has strategic patents acquirer can't risk going to a competitor

Sometimes a double or triple is a great exit for you as long as it doesn't take too long to happen and the company has not raised too much.

Dividends and Royalties

Although relatively infrequent, dividends and royalties are a great way to generate returns

- It can take quite a while before a company has enough cash to fund a dividend payout
- Dividends can accumulate in the background; either simple or cummulative
- Royalty or Revenue-based payments are typically put in place as part of deal structure at the time of initial investment

Revenue based financing provides early liquidity, but can harm growth. Dividends tend to hold management's feet to the fire as they shift value from common to preferred over time.

Stock Buy-outs and Buy-backs

Tend to come in two different flavors

- **Company** buys shares from investors interested in selling (buy-back)
- Expect limited return to investors in this scenario

- New investor, typically a large VC, wants to buy more stock than company is willing to sell (buy-out)
- New investor offers to buy shares from current investors

Buy-backs are associated with slow-growing profitable companies; buy-outs are associated with rocket ships, and can be really tough "liquidity vs upside potential" decisions.

Large Acquisitions

By far the most common type of big exit for angels

- Expect will take many years since it takes time to build the kinds of things a major acquirer pays big money for
- Acquisition usually includes large payment and a smaller (10-25%) escrow payment 12 to 18 months in future

Really big exits are much less common and can take many years of patient growth.

Successful IPOs

An IPO is the Holy Grail of angel investing

- IPOs are a rare beast these days
- Companies are staying private much longer
- Mezzanine funds, hedge funds, and private equity are active financiers for most, if not all, of a growing company's capital needs

An IPO in your angel portfolio will not only give you awesome bragging rights for years to come, it will almost certainly ensure overall portfolio success.

ANGEL FINANCE
Timing and Planning Exits

How to Plan Exits

Management and the board need answers to the following

- Who might buy the company?
- Why they might buy the company?
- What they might value the company for?
- What milestones have to be reached before there is interest?

Getting answers to these questions should come up during due diligence and be a recurring topic at board meetings.

What are the Initial Steps in the Exit Process?

Build CEO and senior executive relationships with key industry players

Look for opportunities to establish industry thought leadership

Keep corporate records scrupulously organized and up-to-date

If you run your company like you might be approached by a buyer tomorrow, you know you will maximize your chances of being ready when the opportunity arises.

How Do You Find the Right Acquirer?

Start by answering the question: "Who are the top 5 potential acquirers for this company, and why might they think it is valuable?"

Are the acquirers in different categories with different motivations?

Then, build relationships with likely buyers and key industry players

Where appropriate, establish partnerships to help grow sales and position the company for an exit

Experienced investors understand the important distinction between "selling" your company and having someone "buy" your company.

Who are the Key People at the Acquirer?

The primary decision makers in a strategic acquisition include:

- CEO, Division General Manager
- Corporate Development & Legal
- Key senior team leaders in product and sales

M&A is a lot more like romance than a military campaign, though it has elements of both.

Attributes of Strategic Acquirers

An operating company looking to acquire a target company's customers, technology, people, marketshare, etc.

Strategics see potential to reap significant benefits from putting two companies together

Rightly or wrongly, strategic buyers are often willing to pay more than financial buyers for a company.

Attributes of Financial Acquirers

Private Equity is the most common term used to categorize these acquirers

They are philosophically money managers and cash harvest operators, not growth company operators

They rarely overpay for a company since their financial model is based on harvesting cash and reselling the company in a few years for a quick return

Beware the PE acquirer who does not want to buy the whole company at once. Some like to buy only part at first as a way of tying up less cash.

What Does an M&A Timeline Look Like?

Most deals take at least 6 to 9 months from initial contact to close

Longer timelines are associated with:

- Lack of seller readiness for the process
- Lack of buyer conviction or competition between multiple buyers
- Complex deal structuring issues like tax issues, strategic shareholder approval issues, key regulatory approvals, etc.

The above timeline doesn't start UNTIL the board has decided to go, hired a banker and actually engaged with potential acquirers!

How Should Management Prepare?

Have good advisors either on the board, in the investor base, or from an outside banker

Have clear delegations of responsibility for different aspects of the process

Train senior management to stay on script with key messages

Understand the importance of speed and responsiveness - these windows to do not stay open long

Nobody is born knowing how to do M&A well - get help or you can fumble at the one yard line and ruin the returns you have worked years to earn.

Openings in the Exit Window

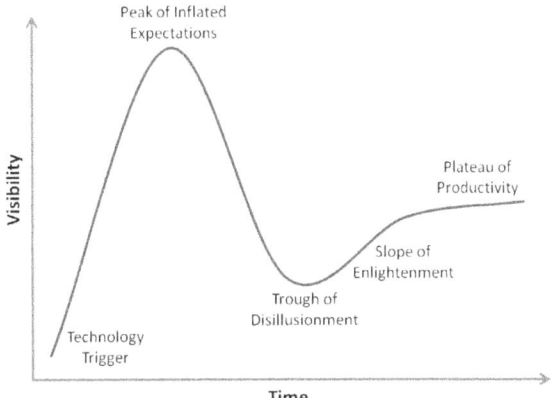

The Gartner Group Hype Cycle graph is a great indicator of value inflection points for a company.

Failing to Capitalize on Open Exit Windows

Failure by a CEO and the board to act on a good exit offer typically occurs for one of the following reasons:

- The board doesn't recognize the offer for how good it is
- The company is not ready to act quickly enough
- There is misalignment with the board and management team

Boards should regularly discuss with management what the MAD or "minimum acceptable deal" is and understand that at all times.

Are There Other Reasons for No Sale?

Too much capital was invested, and so some investors can't get the multiple needed to achieve their financial goals and balk, hurting other investors

Expectations for valuation are too high

Too much competition and the company isn't well positioned to command a premium sale price

CEO enjoys running the company and is not willing to let someone else take control
Acquirer's plans to move, terminate or demote employees

There are a million ways an acquisition can go wrong - take every credible offer seriously, and coach management that it is a marathon, not a sprint.

ANGEL FINANCE
Alignment

Different Teams and Kinds of Investors

Founding teams vary:

- Some like the early years and just want to put a few million $$ in their pocket and repeat
- Some want to build long term and run a massive company

Investors vary:

- Some angels favor early exits, some want to go for it
- Early stage VCs are looking for grand slams
- Growth stage VCs are looking for 3-5x
- Late stage VCs and Institutions want a fast 2-3X

There is no right answer; everyone needs to make sure they are on the train that gets them to their destination.

Management and Investor Alignment Issues

Management and investors are both looking to build a company that delivers significant shareholder value

But, misalignment frequently occurs in the following situations:
- Minimum acceptable size for an exit
- Acceptable timing and plan in place for an exit
- Size and deal terms around future rounds of financing
- Treatment of employees

Alignment should be discussed and verified at the first round and revisited with every single additional step along the capital path.

Limiting the Likelihood of Misalignment

Whether you are a board member or a key investor, you should:
- Establish long term financing plan designed to meet company goals
- Discuss long term implications of raising additional rounds of financing
- Confirm that new investors have similar expectations for future financing
- Discuss potential exit scenarios that are acceptable to all parties

Angels should be proactive and have these discussions with management early on when their relative influence is greatest.

How Do You Get Back on Track?

Lack of regular communication is main culprit for creeping advancement of misalignment

Board should discuss on an annual basis the long term financial plan

Plan needs to address key issues such as future financing and exit strategy

With each new round of financing, carefully review deal terms that most closely impact your returns. Work with the board to negotiate out the most egregious deal terms that can lead to future misalignment issues.

ANGEL FINANCE
Appendix

Resources - Exit Planning

Most early stage companies return maximum value to their shareholders through some form of acquisition. Planning for such an exit is an ongoing responsibility for both the CEO and the board. With that challenge in mind, we put together a guide to help with this planning exercise. CEOs should use this guide as an approach or checklist to help stay on top of who their potential acquirers are and what the company's relationship is with each acquirer. And, furthermore, CEOs should use this guide as a way to update the board on at least an annual basis.

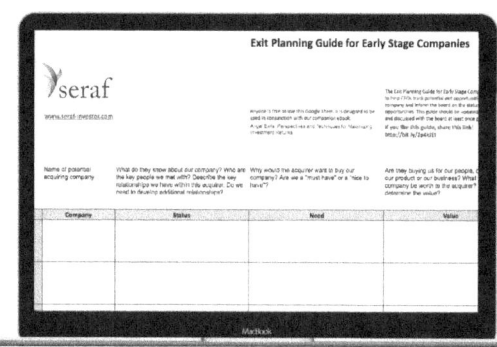

Download Guide
bit.ly/ExitPlanningGuide

Resources - Capitalization Tables with Waterfall Analysis

If you perform a Google search for the term "Cap Table", you will end up with dozens of tools to choose from. These options include everything from Excel spreadsheets that build simple cap tables all the way along the spectrum to complex, high-end software products. We built ones we think you might prefer.

1. We wanted a tool that was very simple to set up. We didn't want to have to enter lots of data to model a cap table.
2. We wanted a tool that allowed us to model a variety of different exit scenarios to help understand how much each shareholder would get depending on the size of the exit.
3. We wanted a tool that was free for everyone to use with no strings attached.

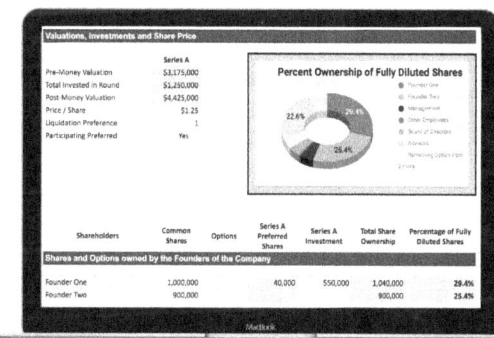

Download Tool
bit.ly/Series_A_and_B_Cap_Table_and_Waterfall

The Seraf Compass

Continue Your Angel Education and Improve Your Investing Skills

The Seraf Compass guides early stage investors in making better investing decisions, minimizing risk and improving returns

Angel Finance Articles

bit.ly/AngelInvestingByTheNumbers

Angel Finance eBook

bit.ly/ByTheNumbersEbook

Angel Finance Hardcopy Book

bit.ly/HardCopyBooks

Angel Finance Tools

bit.ly/SerafToolbox

ACA
ANGEL CAPITAL ASSOCIATION

seraf

The Seraf Compass

From Investment to Exit: Insights, news, thought leadership and in-depth resources for early stage investors

ACCESS OUR CONTENT

BLOG

BOOKS and eBOOKS

TOOLS

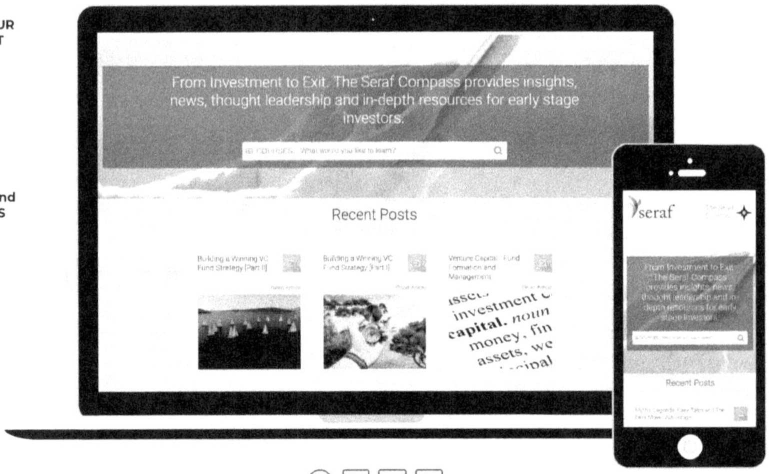

FOLLOW US ON SOCIAL MEDIA

ACA
ANGEL CAPITAL ASSOCIATION

seraf

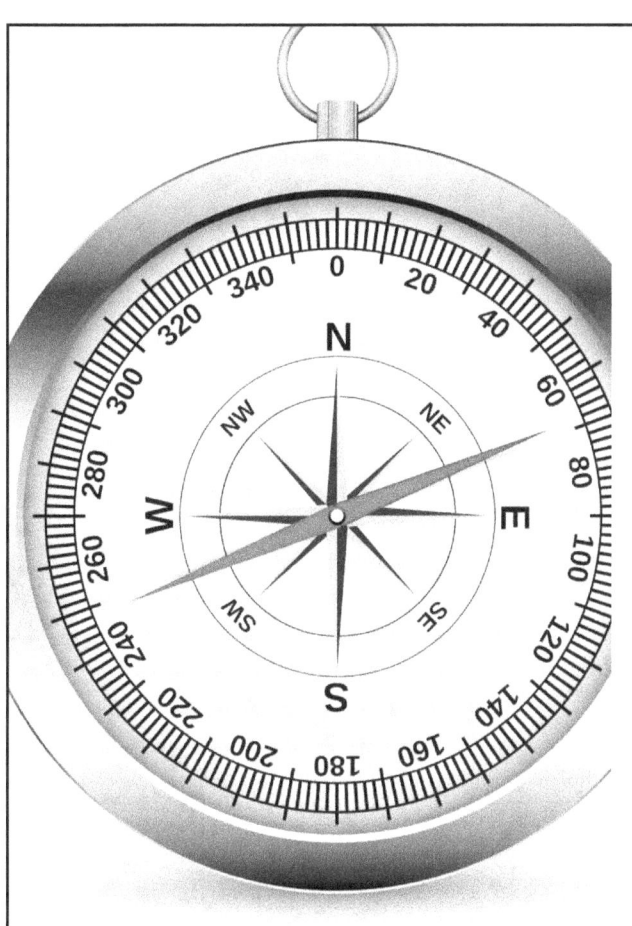

Books from Seraf

Fundamentals of Angel Investing
A Guide to the Principles, Skills and Concepts Every Angel Investor Needs to Succeed

Angel Investing by the Numbers
Valuation, Capitalization, Portfolio Construction and Startup Economics

Leaders Wanted: Making Startup Deals Happen
Advanced Techniques in Deal Leadership and Due Diligence for Early Stage Investors

Guide, Advise and Inspire: How Startup Boards Drive Growth and Exits
An Overview of the Principles, Skills and Concepts Every Early Stage Company Board Member Needs to Succeed

Venture Capital: A Practical Guide
A Guide to Fund Formation and Management

PORTFOLIO MANAGEMENT FOR EARLY STAGE INVESTORS

All Your Info. One Place. Smart Investing.

WHAT MAKES SERAF DIFFERENT

Easy Workflow
Seraf guides you through a few easy steps to get your portfolio up and running quickly. Get an overview, develop insights and generate reports in no time.

Deep Experience
Designed by active, early stage investors with over 25 years experience in fund creation and management, the Seraf team understands the complexities of today's early stage investment landscape.

Uniquely Focused Solution
Developed specifically to meet the needs of early stage investors, Seraf provides the tools YOU need to manage your portfolio efficiently.

AUTHORS

Hambleton Lord

Christopher Mirabile

CONTACT US

www.seraf-investor.com

www.angelcapitalassociation.org

Appendix

In this appendix, we provide a series of templates and guides to help improve your overall investment returns.

Capitalization Table with Waterfall Analysis: This is a collection of two spreadsheets that help you model a company's capitalization table and the resulting waterfall analysis based on a variety of exit scenarios for the company. (https://bit.ly/Series_A_Cap_Table_and_Waterfall or https://bit.ly/Series_A_and_B_Cap_Table_and_Waterfall)

Sample IRS Section 83(b) Election Form: An IRS Section 83(b) Election is an approach to minimizing the amount of tax a director will pay as she vests any restricted stock she received as compensation for board service. We provide a standard form and the necessary instructions so you can successfully file your election with the IRS. (https://bit.ly/IRS_83b_Election_Form)

Early Stage Investment Portfolio Modeling Tool: This spreadsheet allows you to model potential outcomes for the overall return from an early stage investment portfolio. (https://bit.ly/Seraf_Portfolio_Modeling_Tool)

Exit Planning Guide: The startup company IPO is a much rarer creature than it used to be, so most early stage companies return maximum value to their shareholders through some form of acquisition. Planning for such an exit is an ongoing responsibility for both the CEO and the board. With that challenge in mind, we put together a guide to help with this planning exercise. (https://bit.ly/Exit_Planning_Guide)

Versions of each of these documents are available online. If you go to the URL next to each item, you will be able to access an online document that will save you time in creating your own copy of these documents.

Capitalization Tables with Waterfall Analysis

Have you ever been in a situation where you are negotiating an investment with an entrepreneur and you can't agree on the pre-money valuation? Any early stage investor who makes more than one or two investments will certainly run into this issue. It's never an easy discussion, so it helps if you are prepared ahead of time with concrete facts and figures for your recommended valuation. If you do a little homework, not only might you be surprised how little difference small changes in valuation make for founders, you will also be armed to have a very educational discussion with the entrepreneurs.

Let's play out a scenario that Christopher and I ran into recently with a company in which we were looking to invest. At a high level, here are the key facts about the company today, along with a few assumptions we will make about the future of the company.

- The company is pre-revenue and needs to raise $1.25M to get their product shipping and close their first few customer deals.
- We were willing to invest at a $3.6M pre-money valuation. The entrepreneur insisted on a $4M valuation.
- We assumed the company will need an additional $5M Series B financing to get all the way to an exit.
- We assumed the Series B round will be priced at 2X the post-money valuation of the Series A round, and both rounds will be Non-Participating Preferred.
- We assumed that approximately 5% of the common shares are held by employees, directors and advisors.
- We assumed an exit for the company will be somewhere in the $25M to $100M range.

So, given those facts and assumptions, what difference does our requested valuation ($3.6M) versus the entrepreneur's desired valuation ($4M) actually make to the returns of each party?

	$3.6M Series A Valuation	$4M Series A Valuation
$25M Exit		
Founders	$9.3M	$9.9M
Series A Shareholders	$4.6M	$4.3M
$50M Exit		
Founders	$18.7M	$19.7M
Series A Shareholders	$9.1M	$8.7M
$100M Exit		
Founders	$37.3M	$39.5M
Series A Shareholders	$18.2M	$17.3M

Note that our $3.6M pre-money offer is 10% less than the founder's $4M pre-money expectation. The final outcome for the entrepreneur in all of the above exit scenarios shows about a 5% to 6% difference in what they will ultimately receive upon an exit. Even though it feels to the entrepreneur that our respective valuations are miles apart, the reality is about half the difference in the end.

It is probably worth pointing out to the entrepreneur that there are two further advantages for them in keeping the pre-money reasonable:

It makes it easier to bring investors into the round so that they can finish the fund-raising quickly and get back to focusing on the operations of the company. And, it means the post-money valuation will be more reasonable, which means it will be less of a yoke around their necks (see Chapter 2) as they head into the uncertainties that lie ahead and try to grow into justifying their valuation for the next round.

So hopefully you are convinced it is worth doing some modeling. But how can you easily do this type of financial modeling to help better understand valuation and exit scenarios? You need a good Cap Table and Waterfall Analysis tool.

If you perform a Google search for the term "Cap Table", you will end up with dozens of options to choose from. These options include everything from Excel spreadsheets that build simple cap tables all the way along the spectrum to complex, high-end software products that will track everything you need for a complete cap table. But we built one we think you might prefer using.

So why did we bother creating another cap table tool when there are so many options out there? We did it for several reasons:

1. We wanted a tool that was very simple to set up. We didn't want to have to enter lots of data to model a cap table.
2. We wanted a tool that allowed us to model a variety of different exit scenarios to help understand how much each shareholder would get depending on the size of the exit.
3. We wanted a tool that was free for everyone to use with no strings attached.

We chose the familiar Google Sheets platform and created two separate documents. The first sheet allows you to create a cap table with just a single Series A round of financing for very basic modeling.

Valuations, Investments and Share Price

	Series A
Pre-Money Valuation	$3,175,000
Total Invested in Round	$1,250,000
Post-Money Valuation	$4,425,000
Price / Share	$1.25
Liquidation Preference	1
Participating Preferred	Yes

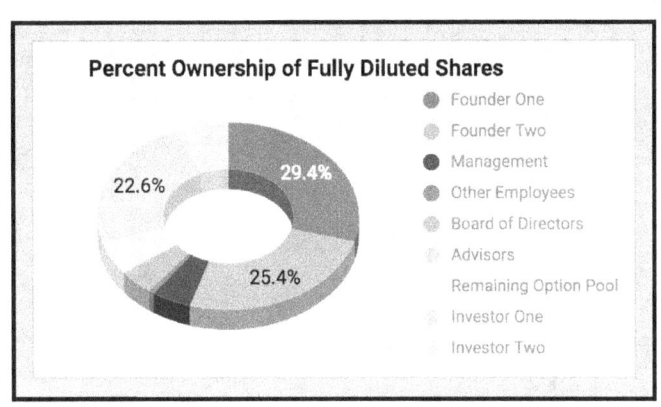

Shareholders	Common Shares	Options	Series A Preferred Shares	Series A Investment	Total Share Ownership	Percentage of Fully Diluted Shares
Shares and Options owned by the Founders of the Company						
Founder One	1,000,000		40,000	$50,000	1,040,000	29.4%
Founder Two	900,000				900,000	25.4%
Shares and Options owned by Employees, Advisors & Directors						
Management	100,000	75,000			175,000	4.9%
Other Employees		25,000			25,000	0.7%
Board of Directors		30,000	120,000	$150,000	150,000	4.2%
Advisors		10,000			10,000	0.3%
Remaining Option Pool		200,000			200,000	5.6%
Shares Acquired by Investors						
Investor One	200,000		600,000	$750,000	800,000	22.6%
Investor Two			240,000	$300,000	240,000	6.8%

Cap Table with a Series A Round of Financing

The second sheet allows you to create a cap table with both a Series A and Series B round. In both sheets, we provide a waterfall analysis so you can model exactly how much capital is returned to each shareholder and each class of stock under a variety of exit scenarios.

These sheets were designed with a fairly common capitalization structure in mind. The sheets support the following key features:

- Either one or two rounds of Series Preferred Stock
- Participating and Non-Participating Preferred Shares
- Liquidation Preferences
- Options, both Issued and Non-Issued
- Waterfall Analysis to model multiple exit scenarios

Summary Cap Table

Security Type	Outstanding Shares	Price per Share	Liquidation Preference	Percent Ownership
Common Shares	2,200,000			66%
Issued Options	140,000			4%
Series A Preferred Shares - Participating	1,000,000	$1.25	$1,250,000	30%
Total Shares Outstanding	3,340,000			

Exit Proceeds

	Price	Price	Price	Price
Purchase Price for the Company	$2,000,000	$4,175,000	$10,000,000	$20,000,000

Liquidation Preference Calculation

Series A Liquidation Preference	$1,250,000	$1,250,000	$1,250,000	$1,250,000
Remaining Proceeds	$750,000	$2,925,000	$8,750,000	$18,750,000
Proceeds per Common Share	$0.22	$0.88	$2.62	$5.61
Proceeds per Series A Share (as converted)	$0.22	$0.88	$2.62	$5.61
Total Proceeds per Series A Share	$1.47	$2.13	$3.87	$6.86

Returned Capital by Round

Common Shares	$494,012	$1,926,647	$5,763,473	$12,350,299
Options	$31,437	$122,605	$366,766	$785,928
Series A Preferred	$1,474,551	$2,125,749	$3,869,760	$6,863,772
Total Proceeds	$2,000,000	$4,175,000	$10,000,000	$20,000,000
Series A Return Multiple	1.2	1.7	3.1	5.5

Waterfall Analysis with a Series A Round of Financing

It's also important to note that for the sake of simplicity and usability these sheets are NOT designed to support the following items commonly found in cap tables:

- More than two rounds of Series Preferred Stock
- Convertible Notes
- Dividends
- Warrants

So, if you are looking for a complete solution that will help you manage every aspect of your company's cap table, just do a Google search and you will find plenty of great products to purchase. In the meantime, try out these free Google sheets to help you build a well structured cap table along with a waterfall analysis for exit scenario modeling.

Sample IRS Section 83(b) Election Form

Many years ago I joined the board of a company after my angel group became the lead investor in the company's seed financing round. As part of my compensation for being a board member, the company issued me restricted stock. Since I was new to the early stage investing world, I didn't understand what the tax implications were with restricted stock. It's unfortunate that I didn't get good tax planning advice at the time, because if I had, it would have saved me a significant amount on my tax bill when the company was acquired for a very significant price!

Fortunately, you don't have to make the same mistake I did. To help you avoid my fate, let's get started and provide you with some critical planning advice to help you put better plans in place. After you read this article, you should have a basic understanding of the following items:

- What is Restricted Stock?
- What is an IRS Section 83(b) Election?
- What do I need to do to file an 83(b) Election?
- What are the tax implications when you file an 83(b) Election?

Restricted Stock is given to employees, directors and advisors of early stage companies as a form of compensation. It's called restricted stock because your ownership rights are imperfect or restricted. There may be vesting conditions which need to lapse or there may be "restrictions" on when the shareholder is able to sell this stock. Most restricted stock grants require that the shareholder be active with the company for a certain number of years in order to fully own all of the restricted stock.

An **IRS Section 83(b) Election** is an approach to minimizing the amount of tax you will pay as you vest your stock. What you are basically doing is opting to pay taxes earlier than you have to (1) to lock in a low value at that time and (2) in exchange for a better rate later on. In effect, you declare ownership early, and pay ordinary income taxes on your ownership when the stock is less valuable and then later pay the lower capital gains tax rate on the increase in value.

How does this work? In the early days of a startup company, the fair market value of the stock is pretty low because the company isn't worth that much. Over time, the stock becomes more valuable as the company grows its revenues and builds value for its shareholders. Since restricted stock is treated as income by the IRS, it's best to recognize that income on your taxes when the company's stock is at a low value. Filing an 83(b) Election is allowing you to recognize, by approval of the IRS, the value of the restricted stock at the date of the election versus later as the stock vests.

Filing an 83(b) Election is not that complicated, but it does require a fair number of steps and it must be done in a very timely fashion. The first thing to be aware of is you must file your 83(b) Election **within 30 days of receiving the grant**. That's not much time to get your paperwork filed, but those are the rules! Now, here are all the steps you must take to make a proper election…

- Start by downloading a Sample IRS Section 83(b) Election Form. There are a few items you will need to know to fill out the form, including the fair market value price of the shares you are receiving and the total amount of income that will be added to your gross income.
- If you download this sample form, you will also notice a sample cover letter that you should fill out and include when you mail your 83(b) Election Form.
- Once you complete the 83(b) Election Form and the cover letter, you should mail them to the IRS Service Center where you typically file your federal income taxes. If you are a stickler about keeping tidy records, you can send your mail by certified mail and request a return receipt.

- **And, make sure you send these documents within 30 days of receiving the grant!**
- The final item on your task list is to mail a copy of the 83(b) Election Form to the company for their financial records.

It's also important that you understand the **tax implications when you file an 83(b) Election**. There are three types of tax rates you need to be aware of to understand how filing an 83(b) will affect the amount of tax you ultimately pay out.

- **Ordinary Income Tax Rate**: For high income individuals (which I assume includes most people who end up receiving restricted stock!), this tax rate is the highest rate you will pay. In 2016, the maximum rate was set at 39.6%.
- **Short Term Capital Gains Tax Rate**: If you sell your stock after holding it for less than one full year, you will pay taxes at the Short Term Rate. In 2016, your Short Term Rate was the same as your Ordinary Income Tax Rate.
- **Long Term Capital Gains Tax Rate**: If you sell your stock after holding it for more than one full year, you will pay taxes at the Long Term Rate. In 2016, the Long Term Rate was 20%.

One goal of filing an 83(b) Election is to limit the amount of taxes you pay while your stock is vesting. To illustrate how an 83(b) Election works for your taxes, let's walk through a very simple example.

You receive a grant of 100,000 shares that are valued at $0.05 per share at the time of the grant. If you file an 83(b) Election within 30 days of this grant, you will need to include $5,000 of income on your taxes for that year. If you are in the highest tax bracket (39.6%), you will pay **$1,980 in Federal Taxes**.

Now, let's say you don't file an 83(b) Election. In this case, you will pay taxes over a four year period as follows.

- To keep this example as simple as possible, I will assume that your stock vests at a rate of 25% each year. So every year, you vest 25,000 shares. And, again to keep this simple, I will assume that the stock appreciates in value each year by $0.05 per share. That's a conservative assumption for a company that's doing reasonably well and showing solid growth.

- At the end of year one, you vest 25,000 shares and the price of those shares is $0.10 at the time of vesting. Your income for the year is $2,500 and you pay $990 in Federal Taxes (39.6% of $2,500).

- At the end of year two, three and four, you vest 25,000 shares each year. The price of the shares is $0.15 at year two, $0.20 at year three and $0.25 at year four. Your income for each of those years is $3,750, $5,000 and $6,250. And finally, your Federal tax payments are $1,485, $1,980 and $2,475.

- All told, you will pay **$6,930 in Federal Taxes** during the four year vesting period.

In this example, by filing an 83(b) Election, **you saved $4,950** on your Federal Tax bill. Not a bad savings for a few minutes of work!

There's one other potential large tax savings if you file an 83(b). That savings relates to a reduction of the Long Term Capital Gains tax you pay when holding stock for more than five years. This significant tax reduction is described in IRS Section 1202 of the US Federal Tax Code.

It's possible to pay no Long Term Capital Gains on your Federal tax return for stock held more than five years. By paying taxes on your restricted stock when you first receive the grant, you start the clock ticking on the five year holding period right away. If you wait to pay taxes on the stock at each year of vesting, you push out the five year holding period. So, for example, if the company is acquired 6 years after your initial restricted stock grant, you will pay no Federal capital gains on that stock if you filed an 83(b). If you didn't file an 83(b), you will pay Federal capital gains tax on the stock you vested in years 2, 3 and 4. And, that could be a BIG tax hit!!

Beware of the one downside to the 83(b) Election. If the company goes out of business a year or so after you file your 83(b), you will have paid taxes on value you will never receive, and you can't get those tax payments refunded.

Since taxes can be quite complicated, you should talk to your financial advisor / accountant to make sure you are doing the right thing given your personal financial situation.

Sample IRS Section 83(b) Election Form

ELECTION UNDER SECTION 83(b) OF THE
INTERNAL REVENUE CODE OF 1986, AS AMENDED

      The undersigned taxpayer hereby elects, pursuant to Section 83(b) of the Internal Revenue Code of 1986, as amended, to include in his or her gross income for the current taxable year, the amount of any compensation taxable to him or her in connection with his or her receipt of the property described below:

The name, address, taxpayer identification number and taxable year of the undersigned are as follows:

NAME OF TAXPAYER: _____

TAXPAYER'S ADDRESS: _____

TAXPAYER ID#: _____

TAXABLE YEAR FOR WHICH ELECTION IS BEING MADE: Calendar year [Year]

1. The property with respect to which the election is made is described as follows: [Number of Shares] shares (the "Shares") of the Common Stock, $0.0001 par value per share, of [Name of Company], a [State of Incorporation] corporation (the "Company").

2. The date on which the property was transferred is: _____.

3. The nature of the restriction(s) to which the property is subject is: (a) taxpayer shall not sell, assign, transfer, pledge, hypothecate or otherwise dispose of, by operation of law or otherwise, any Shares, or any interest therein, that are not vested; and (b) in the event that the taxpayer ceases to be employed by or provide services to the Company before the Shares vest, the Company shall have the right and option to purchase from the taxpayer some or all of the Shares at a price equal to $0.0001 per share.

4. The fair market value at the time of transfer, determined without regard to any restriction other than a restriction which by its terms will never lapse, of such property is: [$X.XX] per share.

5. The amount, if any, paid by the taxpayer for such property: [$Y.YY] per share.

6. The amount to be included in the taxpayer's gross income is [$Z.ZZ].

The undersigned taxpayer will file this election with the Internal Revenue Service office with which taxpayer files his or her annual income tax return not later than 30 days after the date of transfer of the property. The undersigned will also submit a copy of this statement to the person for whom the services were performed in connection with the undersigned's receipt of the above-described property. The transferee of such property is the person performing the services in connection with the transfer of said property. Nothing contained herein shall be held to change any of the terms or conditions of the award agreement or the plan pursuant to which the Shares were granted.

The undersigned understand(s) that the foregoing election may not be revoked except with the consent of the Commissioner.

Dated: _____   _____

[Name], Taxpayer

The undersigned spouse of taxpayer joins in this election.

Dated: _____   _____

_____, Spouse of Taxpayer

Sample Cover Letter for IRS Section 83(b) Election

Department of the Treasury
IRS Service Center
[Address of IRS Office where you mail your taxes]

To Whom It May Concern:

Enclosed with this letter is an executed original of the IRS Section 83(b) Election under the Internal Revenue Code of 1986, as amended. This Election Form is filed for:

Name: _____

SSN: _____

Sincerely,

[Name]

Portfolio Modeling Tool

One of the biggest challenges faced by early stage investors is to assemble a portfolio of investments that in aggregate return more than 2 times the original amount invested in the total portfolio. In the language of Venture Capital, the goal of a successful early stage investor is to achieve a Distributed to Paid-In (DPI) ratio greater than 2X. In other words, for every dollar you invest in your portfolio, you want to get two dollars back over time. And, if you want to be one of the top decile early stage investors, you want to shoot for a DPI of 3X or greater.

A successful early stage investment portfolio has a mix of strikeouts, base hits and home runs. So how is it possible for an early stage investor to build a successful portfolio compiled from companies that produce such widely different financial returns? To answer that question, we pulled together a simple modeling tool that helps you visualize how the probable returns play out and interact to produce an overall portfolio return. As usual, we built it as a Google Sheet that allows you to make a copy and model a number of scenarios for your own portfolio.

Investment Portfolio

		Type of Exit	Exit Multiple
Total Amount Invested	$500,000	Loss	0
Amount of Capital Returned	$1,335,000	Breakeven	1
Distributed to Paid-In (DPI) Capital Ratio	2.67	Base Hit	4
		Home Run	10
		Grand Slam	25

Individual Investments: Exit Types and Returns

Company Name	Total Investment	Percentage of Portfolio	Type of Exit	Total Amount Returned
Investment 1	$25,000	5%	Loss	$0
Investment 2	$50,000	10%	Base Hit	$200,000
Investment 3	$25,000	5%	Loss	$0
Investment 4	$15,000	3%	Base Hit	$60,000
Investment 5	$50,000	10%	Home Run	$500,000
Investment 6	$25,000	5%	Loss	$0
Investment 7	$15,000	3%	Loss	$0
Investment 8	$50,000	10%	Breakeven	$50,000
Investment 9	$25,000	5%	Base Hit	$100,000
Investment 10	$25,000	5%	Breakeven	$25,000
Investment 11	$25,000	5%	Loss	$0
Investment 12	$50,000	10%	Base Hit	$200,000
Investment 13	$50,000	10%	Base Hit	$200,000
Investment 14	$20,000	4%	Loss	$0
Investment 15	$50,000	10%	Loss	$0
Totals	$500,000	100%		$1,335,000

How do you go about using this modeling tool? To start, we created a sample portfolio of 15 companies for you to work from. That's enough companies to begin with for a basic portfolio modeling exercise. For each company, there are two variables that you need to set.

- First, you will need to put in an **amount that you invest in each company**. In a portfolio of 15 companies, you might have the same amount invested in each company. Or, you might decide to distribute your investments in a less even fashion. In the default Google Sheet, we've set up a range of investment amounts. Some companies have as little as $15,000 invested and others have as much as $50,000.

- Second, you will need to chose or "model" the **type of exit for each company** in the portfolio. Here is where you determine the multiple of capital each company will return to your portfolio. Since we are dealing with early stage companies, you will have a real mix of returns. If you want a realistic model that will be predictive of probable real-life outcomes, we recommend that you set approximately half the portfolio to total losses (i.e. no capital returned). The rest of the portfolio can be a mix of moderate successes with maybe one or two bigger wins.

There is one other variable that you can control on this sheet. In the upper right quadrant of the sheet is a section for the Exit Multiple for each type of exit. We provide values for each exit type, but you might want to model using different exit multiples. So feel free to change these numbers to fit your needs.

Once you set the two variables for each company (and make any changes to the Exit Multiples), take a look in the upper left quadrant of the Google Sheet. There are three important metrics that are calculated for you in that section.

1. **Total Amount Invested**: This is the sum of all the investments you made in the portfolio and lists the total.
2. **Amount of Capital Returned**: This is the sum of all the returned capital based on the types of exits you set for each company.
3. **Distributed to Paid-In (DPI) Capital Ratio**: This represents the multiple of capital your portfolio returns. Remember, a solid DPI is 2 and a top quartile investor will have a DPI of 3 or greater.

As we discuss above, a DPI of 2X is a good target to aim for. And 3X is even better and puts you in league with the best VCs.

One final thought to keep in mind. This tool is helpful to determine your overall multiple of returned capital. However, it does not factor in the amount of time it took for this capital to be returned. As you are building your own early stage portfolio, make sure you watch out for how long it takes to get a return on your capital. If your returns take significantly more than 10 years to appear, your resulting IRR returns will be much less than optimal. You won't earn enough for the risk you are taking and you might be better off investing in the public stock markets!

Exit Planning Guide

As a director on an early stage company board, how do you deliver on your main responsibility as a board member - maximizing shareholder value? And, what do you do to make sure the CEO is doing her job in increasing the value of your investment in the company? And what good is the increase in value if it is not accompanied by sufficient liquidity to realize it? Those are very important questions that very few early stage company boards take the time and effort to ask early on when it is still possible to have the biggest impact.

The startup company IPO is a much rarer creature than it used to be, so most early stage companies return maximum value to their shareholders through some form of acquisition. Planning for such an exit is an ongoing responsibility for both the CEO and the board. With that challenge in mind, we put together a guide to help with this planning exercise. CEOs should use this guide as an approach or checklist to help stay on top of who their potential acquirers are and what the company's relationship is with each acquirer. And, furthermore, CEOs should use this guide as a way to update the board on at least an annual basis.

What topics are covered in the exit planning guide for early stage companies?

For each potential acquiring company, the guide asks the following questions:

- **Status:** This really goes to awareness. What is the status of any discussions? What do they know about our company? Who are the key people we met with? Describe the key relationships we have within this acquirer? Do we need to develop additional relationships?
- **Need:** Why would the acquirer want to buy our company? Are we a "must have" or a "nice to have"?
- **Value:** What do they value us for and what kind of valuation rubric might they use? Are they buying us for our people, our technology, our product or our business? What might our company be worth to the acquirer? How will they determine the value - as a multiple of revenue or EBITDA; using a buy vs. build vs. partner analysis, or for some strategic reason like keeping us out of the hands of a competitor?
- **Milestones:** What milestones will we need to achieve before the acquirer will be interested?
- **Current Opportunities:** What opportunities do we have to work with the acquirer before an acquisition is made? What actions are we taking on these opportunities?
- **Appetite for Acquisition:** What acquisitions has this company made in the past few years? What price have they paid for these acquisitions?

By answering these questions with some level of detail, you will get a much better sense for what your company needs to accomplish before it's well positioned for an acquisition. Since putting all your eggs in one basket is not a great strategy, you will want to have a list of at least 5 acquiring companies and preferably more in the range of 10 to 15.

What are some of the questions a potential acquirer will ask an early stage company?

Once you reach the point where there is serious interest in acquiring your company, you will need to be prepared to answer some challenging questions. Some of these questions are specific to your company's growth plans, and we expect the CEO and board have been focused on answering these questions for quite some time.

- What are the key metrics you track to understand how your business is growing? How have those metrics been trending over the past year?
- What do you believe is the total addressable market for your business?
- Where do you see the greatest opportunities for growth in your business? What are you doing today to go after those opportunities?
- What companies do you see as your biggest competitors and what do you think differentiates your products from their products?
- How close to your annual plan have you been over the past 8 quarters? How confident are you in your projects for the upcoming 4 quarters?

Other questions will be specific to your willingness to be acquired. The buyer will want to understand your motivations and fit with their company. So be prepared with great answers to the following questions:

- What are your reasons for selling the company?
- What do you see as the most important synergies between our company and yours?
- After we complete the acquisition, what role will the CEO and her management team play in our company?

These two sets of questions are by no means complete. But, they are a starting point that will help you think about what questions are important for a potential buyer of your company. Start with these questions, add some of your own, and make sure the CEO can answer them all in a credible fashion.

Company	Status	Need	Value
Name of potential acquiring company	What do they know about our company? Who are the key people we met with? Describe the key relationships we have within this acquirer. Do we need to develop additional relationships?	Why would the acquirer want to buy our company? Are we a "must have" or a "nice to have"?	Are they buying us for our people, our technology, our product or our business? What might our company be worth to the acquirer? How will they determine the value?

Company	Milestones	Current Opportunities	Appetite for Acquisitions
Name of potential acquiring company	What milestones will we need to achieve before the acquirer will be interested?	What opportunities do we have to work with the acquirer before an acquisition is made? What actions are we taking on these opportunities?	What acquisitions has this company made in the past few years? What price have they paid for these acquisitions?